The Habitat of Progression

Adolph Obasogie

DEDICATION

To Bishop Xavier Obasogie for his uncommon courage.

CONTENTS

ACKNOWLEDGMENTS

To Zion, Jeremiah, Jezreel and Hephzibah ; my unmovable imprints in my pursuit of God.

1 INTRODUCTION

Many People do not like the idea and experience of stagnation but they are hard stuck with the same ideas that got them into the rut in the first place.

Statistics have proven that only 1% of the world's population end up as millionaires and wealthy people, while only a further 1% of the wealthy ever end up as billionaires.

It is evident that there are levels of rut in life and people who escape the rut at a level might end up getting stuck with the rut at a higher level. Considering this a bit further, why is it that not all who become millionaires ever become billionaires?

You will discover answers in this book and as we go on this journey of discovery, you will access the time-honored principles that will get you past the rut in the present and next level of your life!

Chapter 1

The Habitat of Ignorance.

" Insecurity, vulnerability and fear of failure are often viewed in the negative but they can become the catalyst for the unleashing of the genius within you."

A sage declared 'He who knows not and knows not that he knows not is a fool, leave him."

This surmises the dilemma of people who are steeped in ignorance, unaccomplished in life and lack the platform to get their lives on a roller coaster.

Toastmaster extraordinaire-Les Brown had no platform to get past the rut of his speech impediment and ineducability in his teen years. His grade school teacher became the platform for him to get past the rut of an inability to learn and retain knowledge.

Many other individuals in their own experience have got stuck at one point or the other because the lacked the know-how to move past the rut in their lives. There is nothing miraculous that a person in the habitat of ignorance can ever expect unless he begins to acquire the right knowledge and begin to act on them.

The Canadian Mastermind and Guru Builder-James MacNeil is an exemplar when it comes to breaking out of the circle of ignorance to a new world of enlightened and active knowledge.

He has told in countless recounts how he got the teachings of Les Brown and listened to them again and again until they literally fell apart. He never gave up on them rather he got tapes and held them together until his mind grasped the *teachings and beliefs of Les Brown.*

His mind got a hold of the fact that he can be who he wants to be without an excuse of the predicament of never attending college.

He refused to be dissuaded; rather, he got himself into an ecosystem that reminded him of what he can be instead of what he has being!

The Merriam Webster Dictionary defines ecosystem as a "Complex of living organisms, their physical environment, and all their interrelationships in a particular unit of space. "

There is, therefore, no mincing of words when it is reiterated that what and who you surround yourself with have an eternal impact on what you become. James MacNeil would never have got out of his rut if he never regurgitated Les Brown and there would have been no Les Brown without the teacher who instilled a self-belief in him.

To get on the train of progress, you

need to begin to identify and associate with people, ideas and any source that can pull you out of ignorance. For many people, their eureka moment might be the proven works of another and what you never learn you will never know.

"Never forget that until you know, you can never become"

"The things you are passionate about are not random, they are your calling" Anon

Chapter Two

Ever -Learning

Someone I never met declared that "your attitude determines your altitude and latitude in life".

Behavioral scientists have propounded that your attitude comprises of your beliefs, feelings and other behavioral tendencies.

An attitude is "a relatively enduring organization of beliefs, feelings, and behavioral tendencies towards socially significant objects, groups, events or symbols" (Hogg, & Vaughan 2005, p. 150)

Any wonder that a sage declared

that "who, what, where, when, which and how got me to where I am"

Anyone without the right set of attitude will never get to the zenith of their abilities or potential. It is not rhetorical but a brazen fact of life and it is important you approach life and other endeavors with the right frame of mind.

Most teachers from grade school through the higher citadels are hard pressed to turn away students who take the pain to ask the right questions with the mindset of *learning and acquiring knowledge.*

People in this class end up as the toast of their mentors who will go out of their way to open up a fountain of knowledge for their mentees.

It is oft-quoted that the graveyard is the greatest repository of talents and genius. This is the tragedy of human existence because many people truly have talents and inexplicable genius that can work wonders but they never emerge from the backwaters of wishful thinking. It is never enough to know, what you do with what you know is the game-changer.

Many have been taught that "knowledge is power, but today the thinking is that knowledge is a belief –system and real power lies in your action plan".

Many people go through life hampered by the fear of failure and the perception that they need the approval of certain people around them to get ahead. It is perhaps one of the greatest impediments that hold people back from breaking into new frontiers in their life and business.

Many people become hostages of their circumstances because they fear what people will say when they fail. Why should you ever live your life based on what people say? Others are really held down because they take their inability to meet their targets or attain the heights they set out for as failure. Have you really taken time out to define failure? What people really fear about failure is in what they think it means. For example, it may mean that:

-They have wasted resources

-They won't get the support of those they love

-They will no longer be accorded respect that they used to enjoy

All these and several other reasons define failure for many people.Abraham Lincoln lost the race for the Presidency for a record eight times before he was eventually elected. So, it is important how you view failure and it might be better if you see it as an opportunity to try harder or change course; and not as a proclamation on your abilities.

Attitude therefore is key to moving

ahead in life and pivotal in the habitat of progression. It is worthwhile to remember the saying -' 'if you say you are, then you are''

Chapter Three

Proven Pedigree

''There are so many sounds but few voices''
Anon

The truth is that not many people have the pedigree for evident results, and it is the result of diligent consideration to come across anyone worthy to be so ascribed with a proven pedigree.

There are accomplished people in every field of human endeavor, and every accomplished person got to that height with the help of some other accomplished person or persons. Anyone who is yet to outlast some seasons of life cannot be said to have a proven pedigree. Why some may differ, I have over the years carved my template to peg a ten years timeframe as the minimum threshold to assess when considering a person's pedigree.

This is by no means cutting off people with rapid success or quick results but I realize that ten years is a fairly long time for anyone to learn and reassess his triumphs and failures in any field of human pursuit.

A person that has pursued a focus

and attained evident heights in a profession, vocation or trade is worthy to be said to have a proven pedigree. To get continuous results over a ten-year period or continue with the strings of successes is no mean feat.

Note that a nothing is secularly defined as perennial if it has not crossed the threshold of two years. So, anyone who can outlast a perennial problem is just on the way to getting a proven pedigree.

In the same vein, people are described as serial entrepreneurs when they have continuously come up with new businesses and ideas that are self-sustaining and progressive.

According to Forbes magazine, serial entrepreneurs are more likely to succeed in ventures than first-time entrepreneurs because their experience has taught them to be persistent in selecting the right industry and the time to start new ventures.

An upstart entrepreneur looking for mentorship will do well to look out for a time-tested serial entrepreneur to be acquainted with as a necessary step in the habitat of progression if he is ever to taste the sweetness of fulfillment.

Never allow sentiments get in your way when deciding on who has a worthy pedigree to be considered of any benefit to your progression.

Results are crucial because they are tangible; they can be seen and measured. African Pentecostal trailblazer Benson Idahosa will be nobody without the likes of TL Osborn and Oral Roberts; without a CusD'Amato , there might never have been a Mike Tyson.

Eyes on the Ball

If you ever meet with people who have proven results or not might be of little significance unless you decide from the start to keep your eyes on the stated objectives.

The goal is important as it represents the basis for what you are doing. The goal is your vision, your stated objectives and without it, you will be like those who are ghost-punching.

Chapter four

<u>Defined Pathways</u>

''There are many pathways but I trust and follow the proven one''

While it might be clear that there is no one cut-out way to personal or business triumph, it is also evident that there are several proven pathways that many and all can learn from instead of trying to reinvent the test tube.

It is commonly agreed that the pathways to fulfillment comes by;

1. Develop on your own

2. Seek out a mentor and follow

suit.

While it is possible to develop on your own, it is also known that it may become a very long journey that might mean several battering and heart –rending encounters.

Whereas, if you go for a mentor, instead of learning the hard way, you are privileged to use your mentor's mistakes and successes as a stepping stone.

The unspoken Zeal

There is nobody that can impose the zeal and drive to become who you want to be on you if as a person you lack the basal aspiration. Truth is, many people have the basal aspiration but fail to climb out into fulfillment because they fail in the other necessary accompaniments.

Mentorship

The concept of mentorship is relevant because many vocations and professions in human experience are perpetuated by this time-honored practice. But you find out that a man who could have the world as his oyster remains on the fringe of his calling and aspirations as a direct result of his refusal to pursue this tenet of a defined *pathway.*

Albert Einstein is reputed to have said that the law of compounding is the eighth wonder of the world. It simply means that A mentored B, B mentored C and if you are C, you become the totality of A and B.

When you seek out a mentor or a mentor seeks you out; be ready to give your all to the dictates of such a sage. What happens is that every mentor is a composite of other mentors as well; as he carries the weight of every lesson and idea that he has learned and proven over the years.

Imagine you were going to work on reinventing the light bulb today; how long will it take you to find out what filament to use or the conduction material to apply? It is the same puzzle in every other area of life. There is nothing absolutely new under the sun rather find out who is the closest description to what you are pursuing and how possible it is to get his attention so you can start your journey into the habitat of progression.

People are also wont to forget that life is in stages so they seem to also fail to realize that at certain levels of growth, they need to move on to new mentors so they can make progress in their onward journey through life. Failure to recognize this is a proven pitfall that stunts the growth process

A kindergarten attendant is a good steward or mentor for the infant but at adolescence, it makes no sense for the individual to remain stuck with the same kindergarten attendant because at that stratum of life, other better placed people should be instructing and guiding the teen towards the next stage of life or adulthood

Humility

Humility is an eternal trait and value which anyone who desires to get past the sentry at the habitat of progression must cultivate. People easily can sense the kind of air that you carry along, and it does not matter how much you try to hide it. It becomes evident sooner than later.

An ancient allusion describes the point of pouring water from one vessel into another. It is the practice of emptying one to fill the other. For this to be possible, one of the vessels must be tilted why the other must be placed in a lower pedestal otherwise, the emptying will be useless, and no transfer can take place.

I have noted many gifted people in my more than twenty years as a player in corporate and other stratified circles and this singular trait has been a defining factor when it comes to going past the rut into the habitat of progression.

One of the greatest boxers of all time is the man known as 'Iron' Mike Tyson and at the age of 21, he set the world record as the youngest heavyweight champion the world has ever known. He got the training and facilities to become a world beater but he lacked the humility to be taught how to manage success.

He made over $300 million USD at the prime of his career but by the time he was 40, all he earned was gone either as a result of sheer splurging or as legal settlement for his exuberance. Imagine that he was careful enough to learn how to manage success; his fortune would have been a lot different at the time he was past his prime and unable to stay competitive as an athlete.

Bonus Section

Outgrowing Your Mentor

The truth about people who get the best results is always that they have a template to follow and a standard to adhere to as they make their way through life. Many people never get past their limitations in life because they never had the advantage of a better example that they can learn from in their pursuit of personal and wholesome fulfillment.

Can You Outgrow Your Mentor?

A man who never had the privilege of working in a multinational might never understand the dynamics of working with a transnational team and the likely challenges to overcome in such corporate settings. A millionaire can mentor you to your first millions but growing the millions into billions is a different culture and set of challenges. If this wasn't so, then every millionaire given the pedestal, time and resources will find it easy to become billionaires also but prevalent statistics show otherwise. To make progress along proven directions or set targets don't happen by chance as they are the resultant effects of structured plans and predetermined outcomes. Anyone who never had the exposure to organized work environments, tactical, operational and strategic plans cannot easily do well in a demanding work environment. The Bill Gates of this world made innovations to existing platforms and got rewarded for their efforts but to grow their organizations, they needed to bring in people schooled in the organizational template of managing resources.

When is a Mentor Needed ?

Everyone needs guidance in one form or the other and while this might not be so easily recognizable, it is but a very central theme to life and making progress. A mentor is not just anyone you are fortunate to come but someone with a proven and recognizable mettle in your field or area of interest in life, career or vocation. The privilege of working with a mentor is such that he has walked in your area of aspirations, or has perpetuated results that you also desire as an individual or professional. The biggest challenge for many includes;

- Recognizing that they need a mentor
- Choosing a fitting mentor
- Knowing when to get a new mentor

1.Who Needs a Mentor?

Everyone who desires to get ahead in life and in every stage desires to have a mentor. When kids are growing up, they are sent to kindergarten and preschool where they begin to learn how to relate with people and comportment on a gradual basis. The wardens or teachers become the first mentors to these kids and they begin to repeat and say the signs that they are taught in their learning centres. This perhaps explains in basic terms what the concept of mentoring is all about. However, on a larger scale, just as the kids begin to learn new things and appreciate approach to life, so also do people in every facet of life need a mentor to spearhead and help them understand the approach to making progress in their chosen field. People need to understand that for everything they choose to become or excel in, there are others who must have trudged the same path .

2. Who is a Fitting Mentor

A fitting mentor is not just anyone who has walked a path you are trudging towards but a person with proven results and unassailable experience. Experience really matters here but what is desirable is experience that has perpetuated tangible results. Using the Bible example, Moses led the Israelites into the wilderness but he never had the developed experience of leading a people during his stay in Pharaoh's palace or his sojourn in the land of the midianites. It took Jethro, a man with practical leadership experience among the midianites, to let him know how leadership can be efficient through the devolution of power and assignment of responsibilities. From the pages of scriptures, we also know that David had the privilege of working with Saul and from close range; he did experience life and royalty as well as know from a close how not to be king over a people. The mechanism of mentorship is a great platform to be adequately equipped to sprint into the success you desire. It is also fitting to note that anyone who is not knowledgeable or proven in your area of aspiration will be a misfit in your mentorship goals.

3. Getting a New Mentor

It is important to know that relationships are to be cultivated and everyone that has helped you on your way to the direction you desire should be appreciated. Some people make rapid changes in life and others don't. Those who desire to have the results they have never recorded have to do the things they have never done before. It is also needful to pinpoint that getting better results is always not as result of hard work   but getting acquainted with vital facts.

A professional who has exceeded expectations in his chosen field needs a mentor if he is transiting to the status of an entrepreneur and this is huge.

Most professionals are functional experts and they excel at a segment or a given sphere in the organizations they work. To move into the entrepreneurial sphere, they need to acquire skills and the necessary entrepreneurial edge to succeed. Working with a mentor helps to demystify some seemingly intractable knots that hold the key to entrepreneurial excellence. Formal education provides an overview of learning and understanding of the basis and body of knowledge but mentorship lays bare the proven paths to repeated success and the navigational skills that will help put you through the rough edges and uncertainties.

Many have also failed in their bid to transit to the next phase of aspiration because they took for granted that every phase comes with its own challenges and those who have been there know what works as differentiated from what might work. A millionaire who is keen to transit to a billionaire status needs a billionaire mentor if he must accomplish his goals and perpetuate his billions.

"It was pride that changed angels into devils; it is humility that makes men as angels." Saint Augustine

"True humility is intelligent self-respect that keeps us from thinking too highly or too meanly of ourselves. It makes us modest by reminding us how far we have come short of what we can be". Ralph W. Sockman

Chapter 5

<u>Persistent Pursuit</u>

"He has not failed until he stops trying"

It is often spoken that he who stops reading starts dying and the only way to get to distant shores is to lose sight of the foreshore. The drive and desire to keep up the pursuit of your aspirations or vision is a crucial ingredient for enlistment into the habitat of progression.

Anyone who has lost the desire to move ahead cannot make further progress, and there is no way of putting this mildly. Warren Buffett, the acclaimed most successful investor on earth makes a big buzz about persistence, and this quote makes it clearer.,

"P is for Persistence! Nothing in the world can take the place of persistence. Wishing will not; Talent will not; Genius will not; Education will not; Persistence is like a Genie that creates a magical force in your life."

— Lucas Remmerswaal,

Persistence makes it possible to keep up with the demands of life and its ensuing challenges. No man goes through life without the barbs been hauled at him from all corners.

The habitat of progression is not for

people who expect all things on a platter of gold. Kids have the entitlement mindset, but adults are better placed to know that many things in life function by the mechanism of cause and effect. If you feel life's pressures are too overwhelming for you then you lose the motivation to continue to get past the opposition.

Oprah Winfrey once described how in a particular year all she seemed to know was how to lose money and all things she got involved in was either in disarray or produced sub-optimal results. She reminded herself she was meant to deliver a keynote address at Harvard at the turn of the year. She decided she was going to fight her way back and turn on the coloration of success. That was the season her 'O network' got the needed ratings and slowly but surely, she was back to winning ways.

You can deduce from this that down-seasons come to everyone and everybody face challenges no matter the pedestal of life they find themselves at any point in time. She refused to give up and gave it all a big fight such that at the time she was delivering the Harvard address, she had got her groove back.

Thomas Edison was reputed to have said that he found out 99 times how not to make the incandescent light bulb and not that he failed 99 times in his attempt to make it.

No matter what it is that you regard as your challenge or the pursuit that is of utmost importance to you, remember that those who have set world records or won the biggest laurels all persisted until they got the results that they desired.

Winners they say don't quit, and quitters never win!

The Habitat of Progression

Chapter Six

Your Relationships

''Two is always better than one, when one falls the other can pick him up''

No matter whom you are and where on the earth you were born, there are people who have made vital inputs into your life that becomes a part of your life's story. Everyone was born by someone; raised by someone and nurtured through the stages of life by other people.

The brood you are with helps to define what shapes your beliefs, perception and ultimately your paradigm. Often, it is said that birds of a feather, flock together. It even becomes more than a just an observation when you find that it is easier to find a scholar amongst scholars than amongst any other brood. Knowing this and with a good grasp of the realities of relationships, it will be safe to note that whom you hang out with is as crucial as what you eat, drink or believe.

People who grow up without good parentage always find it harder to become successful in their lifetimes and this is absolutely factual. It is documented that more than 90% of inmates in American prisons are from single parent homes and most never had the privilege of growing up with a father figure in their life.

Loving Relationships

Everyone desires to be loved and it is innately human to crave a loving relationship. This goes a long way to provide stability, a sense of worth and an unmistakable camaraderie.

A Loving Partner

People who have the affection, warmth and the presence of a

loving partner in their life are able to get a boost in fulfilling their desired goals and take on life's challenges. Behavioral studies have shown that the desire to be loved is a motivating presence in every life.

Everyone who has the benefit of a loving experience is able to find a boost as a necessary push for making progress. The effect of a destructive filial relationship can also be devastating but without doubt, those who use the love advantage get ahead assuredly.

Peer Power

The advancement in learning and self-development has over the last two decades brought about Continuous Professional Development programs and modules across the globe. Professionals are generally required to undergo modules of annual or periodic programs to enhance their delivery and practical skills.

Predominantly, this has covered a wide range of professions and increasingly has become the norm. This practice has been so widely accepted that individuals who are unable to meet with the minimal benchmark or accrue the required points are either made to lose license rights or some form of censure.

This push for continuous development is not necessarily a licentiate requirement as much as it is a drive to help professionals remain on the cutting –edge of specific career goals and best practice. Individuals without a structured membership of a career association can also on their own seek out seminars, workshops or training avenues to ensure that they make the best of this progression pill.

<u>Remarkable Advantages:</u>

1. *Easier platform to uphold required benchmarks and disseminate new developments*
2. *Standardization of practices and norms*
3. *A chance for accountability*
4. *Good avenue to compare notes and share experiences.*

"Whoever and whatever increases the order in your life enhances your productivity and self-worth; keep them close"

Chapter Seven

The Team Factor

" I will rather work with two and be known than to work alone and remain obscure"

Not all teams can be effective and efficient in attainment of individual success. A good team with a hierarchy and a decision making system ensures quick and efficient reactions to different challenging situations. Team members are also respected for their expertise and input as this leads to cohesiveness and building of specific characteristics that are vital for efficiency and high individual performance. A team that focuses on individual success should have;

- **A team leader:** who guides and ensures all team members are informed of their duties and responsibilities to attainment of goals. He also governs the approach of team members on various projects, pays attention to varied ideas and ensures the team is well organised and focused into meeting objectives.

- **A team maven:** with wealth of knowledge and proper understanding of the subject matter, a team maven provides readily required information and essential expertise important in achieving desired success.

- *A team realist:*in any team, team members tend to be enthusiastic and sometimes set unachievable individual targets. It is up to the realist to ensure that each person is focused on the objectives and no time is wasted in chasing unrealistic goals

- *A team communicator:* it is up to the team communicator to ensure effective interaction of team members and other important personalities that may be available from time to time. Any arising misunderstanding in a team should be resolved by a team communicator

- **A team supporter:** the role of a team supporter is to ensure team players are not discouraged in meeting set goals and objectives. He encourages, boosts morale and provides support to every *individual in maintaining focus on the task at hand*

For a long time now, team work has been the driving force not only of individual success but also innovation and every other aspect of development. Whether it's in major corporations, countries or even businesses (both large and small), teamwork has always been key to growth and quality outcomes.

When an individual involves himself in a team with all the above aspects, he is likely to achieve more than he can do alone. In a team, one becomes more effective, thoughtful and efficient thus more accomplishments and long term success.

On a personal level, the following are advantages of a team in achieving success;

I. Increased Efficiency

Different people have different specialities. When in a team, each person focuses on what he/she can do best. Specialization and improved team relationships lead to better team rhythm that enhances improved productivity and efficiency. Apart from cost saving, a group approach also helps in meeting set targets in a short span of time

II. Improved Performance

Due to the fact that one only engages on what he/she can do best, the output is of the quality desired and is attained in the most efficient manner with least resources. Important tasks beyond one's capabilities are easily taken care of by more skilled persons

III. Crisis Mitigation and Efficient Problem Solving

No matter how much the

preparation is setbacks may sometimes be experienced. A good team should be able to withstand the inconveniences and the associated stress. As an individual it is difficult to wade through such 'storms'. Team members provide support thus easy tackling of any arising difficult situation.

Coming up with the best solutions to go about a crisis can be overwhelming. However, with team members, it simply means 'more hands on deck' thus attained solutions in short time durations.

IV. Improved Competency

Collaboration helps one maintain focus on his/her core competencies. By being involved in a team, an individual inevitably learns from what others do thereby gaining much more understanding on any relevant subject matter.

V. Improved Trust and Relationships

Trust is bedrock for any success to be attained through teamwork. Coordination with trustworthy and transparent friends improves morale and opens proper channels of communication for information considered vital for growth and development.

Apart from trust, team work not only ensures people are invested in a particular project but also in each other. Members to a team will always support each other even outside the project structure. This eventually leads to sharing ideas that are sometimes important in achieving personal/individual set goals

VI. Reduced Stress

When one is engrossed too much in attaining individual success without involving even the closest of persons, tension builds up and stress takes over. Stress affects mental and physical health therefore productivity. It is therefore considered very vital to have friends and teammates who will ease off pressure by helping you revitalize and re-energize thereby restoring initial vigor.

VII. Maintained Focus

Success cannot be attained if much time is spent on inconsequential matters that do not in any way *contribute to attainment of the overall objective. With focused team members, one maintains eyes on the big picture without losing the overall goal trajectory. Working as a team ensures unified commitment towards achieving set targets*

VIII. Improved Service and Innovation

Strong team spirit, improved collaboration and positive attitude favours better outlay in terms of services. Consequently, in major occasions, innovation results from people who work hard together rather from an individual. For successful innovation, different parties have to be involved for different intrinsic ideas.

The fact that there are different approaches to a project makes team members contribute on different pros and cons of each approach. With this collaboration, the best approach to a project is considered thus overall team success achieved unlike when working as an individual.

Other benefits of a team to achieving individual success include;

- Collaboration of different skills resulting to creativity which could otherwise not be reached by an individual

- Provision of a good supportive environment through which projects are completed and goals easily accomplished

- *available pool of ideas and sharing of expertise thereby understanding different approaches and points of view*
- *Maintaining focus for longer since workload is shared and stress reduced. It is also more satisfying to be part of a bigger project*
- *Utilizing individual strengths for better solutions to emerging challenges thus improved implementation*

- *ensuring compensation on weaker areas since members use the teamwork opportunity to improve on various aspects*

As a member to a team, you will be more motivated to achieving individual success which will contribute to the overall success of the team. Achieve those individual milestones by being part of a team

Chapter Eight

The Networking Advantage

"When one tells two and two tells four, then the planet is covered"

Most people misunderstand networking as merely an exchange of business cards at a party. As per experts, networking involves building of relationships based on trust. It is also incomplete without the give and take aspects i.e. one party conveys information about who he/she really is and the available opportunities while you listen and provide channels that are essential in helping him/her achieve set goals. In the current evolving world, networking is not an option but an important skill to master

Once the networking skill is mastered, broader networks are created and better teams created. Engagements are also built and a *more appropriate work environment created. In the long run, productivity is enhanced*

Networks consist of professionals with similar interests. To benefit from a networking group, members should develop a skill of willingness in the exchange of information and contacts. Members should also be knowledgeable, well connected and with invaluable experience that is in sync with your goals.

When to network

In a working setup, Employees build relationships that will enable them accomplish specific tasks. The same applies to leaders who want specific jobs done. They therefore rely on both internal and external networks so as to accomplish their missions.

Establishment of both internal and external networks by leaders sometimes requires much input in terms of resources. Desired network systems need proper management for effective collaboration efficiency and positive rewards

Do not wait for a crisis to strike then you start building your networks. Initial establishment of networks is always essential in building and maintaining of a professional relationship in the workplace or other relevant companies thus ensuring career advancement and attainment of goals. Always establish networks not with a lot of people but the right ones who can make things happen.

Effective networking to goal advancement

According to surveys conducted, most people with proper networking channels end up fulfilling their goals compared to their counterparts who do not. In seeking to advance goals through networking, it is important to;

- *Set achievable goals and have a strategy of achieving them*
- *Seek a role model/mentor to offer guidance*
- *Always appreciate others with a smile and a word of 'thank you'*
- *Always leave a good first impression*
- *Establish professional follow-ups as soon as possible*
- *Learn the art of paying attention to whatever is said, also gain trust and learn to trust*

others. consequently provide suggestions or different ways of going about an issue

- be confident and think of yourself as a resource
- Be approachable and ready to engage. This can be through business cards and worn name tags as free advertisements. people tend to approach the person they know
- Have an email signature

It is also important not to;

- *Ask for assistance but instead seek professional advice*
- *Be afraid of asking questions*
- *Be selective on your contacts. Strike conversations with co-workers and every other person/colleague in the event*
- *post anything on social media that will convey you negatively*
- *be with anyone who makes you feel intimidated or uncomfortable*

- *Jump in with your offer. Instead maintain your focus on the other party. Get to learn more about their businesses and how you can be of help. This will be essential in building rapport.*

- *Cross arms even when bored or tired as it portrays one as unapproachable thus no need to be 'bothered'. It also conveys you as defensive, judgmental, skeptical or nervous.*

- *Assume. The person you have never seen before might end up being a very important lead and resourceful in achieving your goals. Be cordial, warm and receptive. This is important in ensuring important leads don't form any opinion about you.*

Developing a professional network

Before networking, it is vital to set achievable goals then strategize on how to attain them through a well set plan. Networking can either be social or through informal interviewing. Both have the following outline;

I. Developing

In social networking, this can be through volunteering, joining clubs or organizations that have same interests as yours. It enables you establish and grow your contact base.

It is also important to network

through online sources e.g. Facebook and LinkedIn. Again, get to know whether your contacts know particular persons in specific fields of interest and inquire about their availability in making initial introduction.

Unlike in social networking, Informal interviewing involves more of chatting with network contacts. It actually entails a high standard of focus when conversing. At this stage, one is able to obtain all the necessary information that is required in the attainment of initially set goals.

II. Organizing

This involves planning and being part of an organization/club that you will be most involved in. joining many networking organizations is not advisable since your attention will be divided. Moreover, you may not find time and sufficient resources to commit to all of them. Therefore, be a member of one or two networking organizations (in your area of interest) and be fully involved in any undertaking.

In informal interviewing, organizing involves comprehensive research on different ways and approaches of meeting objectives. With prior research, one will have sufficient information through to strike a conversation on a relevant subject with the contact person

III. Practicing follow ups

For successful follow ups, it is important to remember the name of the contact person. Also, with proper organization and data storage regarding to phone numbers, contact information and email addresses among others, stand out by at least making an extra effort through follow ups.

With initial contacts, ensure you

have ideas and relevant stories to share occasionally so as to maintain the relationship. It is also recommended to send email updates and strike conversations which are in line with your goals.

In the current world, achieving anything of utmost significance involves collaboration from all sectors and hierarchical boundaries. Your contact person can be of much significance with regard to *information relevant to attaining goals and obtaining solutions to problems and setbacks. Find the already existing informal networks and build others so as to enhance your ascension in the habitat of progression.*

Chapter Nine

<u>The Place of Tools and Technology</u>

'' Digital innovation is the greatest invention of the last 100 years''

Goals are very important to ascend onto the habitat of progression, without clear goals, it not easy to know when you have arrived at your intended destination. They help one in determining what he/she wants and who they desire to be in the long run.

Technology is very important in keeping one on track and ensuring he is motivated to attaining his goals. The following are different ways on how to use technology to set and meet your goals.

I. Writing and saving your goal list

Writing a goal list is sometimes considered cumbersome since it requires some bit of time. Even though this might be the case, be focused and spare a little time to do your best thinking and come up with your goal list. It is often recommended to use online sources in shaping your goals and making them attainable. Also ensure they reflect your long term vision

With your goals now in writing; save them in a file in your computer/tablet/smartphone, the format should be the one used daily *i.e. excel or Microsoft word*

Keeping goals in an electronic document is very important since the goal list document will not be misplaced and can be easily referred to over and over again. This keeps the goals fresh in your mind and keeps you motivated to working towards achieving them

II. Automation, Dissemination and Scheduling

While trying to use technology to

meet your objectives, it is important to remember that technology cannot attain goals for you but it can only Automate, Disseminate and Schedule. These are important in helping one work on the set goals.

- ***Automation;*** *some tasks can be machine automated e.g. a goal of saving towards retirement can be automated by initiating direct deposits into your savings* account. Use the new technology to your advantage by automating such routine functions

- **Information dissemination;** sharing your goals with your closest friends can sometimes make one accountable and more motivated. Use emails and join online communities or groups with people with almost similar goals and share ideas *while gaining support at the same time.*

- **Scheduling;** *schedule applications in most personal computers, phones and tablets are important in breaking goals into objectives and assigning due dates against each. Project management software is also essential in scheduling since it enables one to come up with important steps required to reach a goal. Other features like* *calendar help in setting definite timelines, while appointments and reminders automatically keeps you updated with regards to approaching deadlines.*

III. Recognize and Celebrate

When it comes to recognition, new technology comes in handy. The progress in meeting initially set goals can be tracked. When a goal is reached, it is important not to delete it, highlight it in bold and against it add a date to act as a reminder of what you did right to achieving it. As a result, celebrate and stay motivated into achieving other goals.

A. RELEVANT SKILLS

Among others, the following are the relevant and most important skills to realization of goals.

I. Action planning skills

Action planning is the ability to

come up with a model through which focus will be maintained to achieve definite goals. Action planning skills enable one to know where he is, where he wants to be (in line to goals) and the correct actions to take in order to get there.

Prioritizing tasks is an important aspect of action planning. It ensures important actions are completed within the set time limit therefore alleviating pressure that comes with setting and meeting objectives.

Good action planning skills consequently enable one to come up with a timetable that has a clear outline and steps that will help in achievement of goals. This saves much time that could have been spent on inconsequential matters that are not in line with the set objectives

Necessary Steps

Planning involves organizing of activities in order to meet a desired goal. New tools and technology enables one to create a strategic plan and to prioritize therefore saving much time that could have otherwise been spent on inconsequential factors not linked to success. With proper planning, one can forecast of future scenarios and adequately prepare on how to react to them. Planning seeks to;

i. **Build alliance with contact persons;** when resourceful contact persons understand your present objectives, they end up playing a key role in the formulation of plans important for future success

ii. **Lob for resources;** whatever resources required for your success, planning is fundamental in obtaining them. It also helps in optimization of available resources

iii. **Maintain focus on the big picture;** the big picture is to have long term success.

Planning enables one not to drift off the set trajectory and to accomplish objectives within the set time limits

iv. **Render information and feedback;** this can be attained through the following tools;

- **Cloud Tools:** Examples include; Dropbox, OneDrive, Box and Google Drive among others. Cloud tools are essential in ensuring that all stored files with success guidelines be tracked and accessed from anywhere. for convenience

- **Calendaring Tools:** For scheduling appointments with contact persons to share ideas on how to attain long-term success. Outlook or Google calendar can be used on

PCs or Synched to smartphones or tablets.

- ***Social Media Sites:*** *Important for sharing information and long term objectives with close friends or contact persons. Connecting with trusted people can be a great motivation especially when experiencing setbacks*

- ***Content Management Tools:*** *By using Word-press. Blogger, Pinterest or even Tumblr to write about your interests, you will meet same minded people to share experiences and success stories.*

- ***News Aggregators:*** *With insufficient time to go through all your daily undertakings that are* *projected to achieving future success, news Aggregators will enable you flip through the headlines thereby saving you much time. A good example is Feedly and Flipboard*

a.Information Security

With new technology, important data and information in relation to action planning, problem analysis and decision making (all vital in attaining success)can be securely stored and protected from hackers and viruses. Accidental alterations can also be averted and disaster recovery ensued

b.Risk Management

The processing abilities of modern computers enable one to capture relevant data accurately for safe storage, risk monitoring and control for proper decision making

II. Decision making skills

Decision making is as important as action planning and team working in the attainment of goals. Correct decisions teach one how to do something while incorrect decisions provide a learning platform of what should not be done.

Before a final decision is made, one should consider alternatives, the expected outcome of each and the resources required. With goals clearly set, ensure you have sufficient information that will help in deciding the correct course of action. Highlight and analyse critical factors and make decisions that will maximize on your strengths thereby reducing threats and taking advantage of opportunities.

III. Problem Solving and Analytical Skills

Realization of goals has never been easy without problem solving and analytical skills. One should be able to evaluate information and different situations, consider different approaches of obtaining solutions and decide on the most appropriate approach.Any arising problem that tends to hinder you from achieving your goals should be viewed as an opportunity for a different logical approach and fresh start. These skills will help you evaluate the problem and come up with both practical and technical solutions thus moving you closer to attaining goals.

Problem solving and analytical skills also help one to identify and define problems, examine options while acting on the set plan and come up with best solutions with the least or no consequences.

IV. Time management skills

Time management skills enable one to set clear attainable goals break the set goals down into discreet steps and review progress as per the action plan. It consequently ensures prioritisation by maintaining focus on important tasks; builds on proper organisation *thereby enabling one avoid procrastination*

B. OTHER IMPORTANT TOOLS

Apart from skills and new technology, the following tools are important in the realization of goals

- **Daytum:** *a detailed way of keeping track of your daily undertakings into meeting specific goals. the habits are* *then presented in a customised report*

- ***Excess spreadsheet:*** *with a spreadsheet data, which is in line with goals, can be entered and viewed in different ways. reports showing the overall trend can also be generated*

- ***Evernote:*** *provides a platform through which your goal information can be tracked and accessed anywhere for convenience*

- **Spring-pad:** *can be customized into setting up a notebook with name 'goals' with daily accomplishments into achieving the overall goal*

- **Pen and paper:** *though considered analogue, most people are comfortable with it. it can be used as a spread-sheet*

Develop the necessary skills and embrace new technology in attainment of goals. Consequently, find tools that you are comfortable with and create daily habits that will help in reaching both short term and long term goals.

Chapter Ten

Why Change is a Necessity

"Those who never accept the necessity of change are left behind"

To change is to transition to a different desired state with an aim of meeting or achieving a given objective. Regardless of anything that happens, change is considered inevitable. In fact, change is steadfast and is the only thing that doesn't change.

Understanding change

Change can create both a positive and negative impact to a person's life or those around. Imagine a pebble thrown in a pond, it ripples affecting the whole pond. The ripples are likened to the effects of change to the surrounding, a good indication that one should always be cognizant of the resulting effects of what is done or not done

The most important thing about change is how it is managed in order to have a positive impact. Resistance to change only but hinders growth in pursuance of life goals. One should, therefore, set achievable goals, adjust appropriately by working outside the comfort zone and mental status quo to attaining them

Most people are reluctant to change because;

• They are risk averse; to be risk averse is to fear for the unknown. At times people do not know whether the outcome of change will be positive or negative, this bothers them and, as a result, become rigid to positively respond to change.

• They fear being distrusted; despite the outcomes, people will trust you more if you are committed and consistent with initial plans. Any change of mind-set or strategies in pursuance of life goals may sometimes portray you as unsure, inconsistent and non-committal to a particular course of action.

• They are comfortable; sometimes people set life goals and lay down plans through which to attain them. Being committed to these plans makes them maintain focus and stay productive despite any form of distraction. To pursue life goals, change may mean doing an extra more than what was done initially or maybe developing new relationships. It may also imply retraining on an important skill or even losing status. In most cases, therefore, people view change as a distraction from the initially set trajectory hence the reluctance in embracing it

Despite the above, one can only thrive if he is not rigid in undertaking new life challenges.

Embracing change and fighting this rigidity can only be possible if;

• You are confident; self-confidence mitigates the fear of change. The best way of attaining self-confidence is through mental rehearsal or visualization

• You anticipate change; you should not be surprised by change. Monitor trends that relate to your life goals and use the acquired information to embrace change

- You have no comfort zones; it is even more difficult to cope with change if you are already in your comfort zone. Be informed and innovative. Also, learn new skills so as to always stay ahead. Challenge yourself through new strategies essential for coping with change

- You can overcome unknown fears; be receptive to change by overcoming irrational fears. Such fears will only make you stressed and uncomfortable when dealing with change. Such fears also make you anxious and associate change to worst happenings. "Self-talk" is important in overcoming irrational fears as it can change a person's beliefs and manage one's emotional reactions in relation to events.

• You can set new life goals; the new life goals should be compatible with changes one is dealing with so as to help in shifting attention from worries that might arise in attaining those goals.

- You are involved in the change process; be proactively involved in the change process. Involvement provides first-hand experience and information. It also provides a platform to influence the process in a way that can benefit you.

Why change is necessary for the pursuit of life goals

Promotes flexibility

According to research, the ability to obtain solutions to changing circumstances has for a long time now been linked to success and positive outcomes. Flexibility to chance is also associated w intelligence and ambition for the future. Therefore, change is not only necessary in the pursuit of life goals but also important to achieving overall success and satisfaction.

Allows for Tactical manoeuvres and strategic planning

We live in an environment where change is inevitable. Because of this, it is important to have a process in place to help in continuous monitoring of the environment or arising situations so as to help in the establishment of strategic plans essential to meeting life goals.

Brings solutions to negative forces

The ability to come up with strategic plans and tactical manoeuvres in different situations is essential in mitigating the unforeseen or projected negative forces that might act as setbacks in meeting life goals.

Creates Contingency systems for success

A rigid person is one who provides similar solutions to different problems while at the same time expecting different positive results. Recognizing and adapting to the demands of different situations by accepting change enables one to use alternative approaches in coming up with solutions to different problems for long term success and attainment of life goals

Reduces the status quo 'comfort zone' mentality

Comfort zones are the biggest hindrances to success. In fact, one cannot thrive when in his comfort zone. You need to break free from this kind of rigidity and get involved in challenging situations that will make you a better person. Learn new skills, set new goals and strategize on how to achieve them. By accepting change, you have accepted to do a little bit more in the meeting your overall life objectives.

Personal Growth

Every time something changes, it becomes a new discovery that offers insight into different aspects of life. Even the changes that did not lead you to where you projected were important life lessons. Consequently overcoming challenges initiated by change only,, but make you a better person

Breaks Routine

Without change, life ends up being boring since you will keep repeating the same things each day. Life without change is extremely boring, predictable, dull and uninteresting.

Improved life values

Change allows for life re-evaluation and thereby viewing things from a different perspective. This improves and reinforces an individual's life values

Change brings new choices for fulfilment and excitement of life, do not resist it but embrace the one that is essential in fulfilling your dreams.

Chapter Eleven

Inspiration is Necessary

"Passion is the fire needed for Inspiration"

Understanding inspiration

Inspiration involves being mentally or emotionally stimulated to work in achieving something

Being uninspired can happen to anyone; During this time, one experiences no happy moments.

You become drained both mentally and emotionally and cannot work on anything enthusiastically. The initial excitement of achieving set goals and dreams vanishes. Any commitment to meeting certain objectives suddenly fades

Even without inspiration, a person still remains active in working to attain unrelated goals. On attaining them, dissatisfaction still takes over (while at the same time the most important objectives remain unattained).

Pursuing set objectives to achieve the overall goal may be easy. What is challenging is the ability to be persistent and consistent in undertaking your daily habits so as to accomplish objectives. One needs to get inspired for maintenance of long-term commitment, drive, passion and determination in order to move rapidly in the advancement of set goals.

For any form of success, inspiration remains vital. An inspired person remains motivated to try one more time even after the last efforts ended in great disappointments.

Even with much effort and total focus to advance on objectives and meeting goals, your internal drive can be affected by a lot of factors e.g. fatigue, unfavorable environment, insecurities, fear and unhealthy relationships just to mention a few. The most important thing to do when in such a situation is to stay grounded, face the problem and remain focused on the ultimate goal.

Regaining enthusiasm and commitment is very easy. The following easy steps will help you remain inspired for advancement in objectives or set goals.

I.   Have it Easy

This can be achieved through readjusting your focus in the

following different ways

Relaxation; Relax by taking in a deep breath and reflect on goals; with anxiety, one cannot think properly. Relaxation helps in relieving anxiety thus ensuring not only physical but also emotional comfort.

After the desired comfort levels have been attained, reflect on your set goals and different ways of achieving them.

Not pressuring oneself; pressure comes with too many thoughts about something. In fact, it is important to give yourself some space by finding something else to do. Go for a walk, write a poem or try singing if you enjoy it.

Consider this scenario; you are stressed up because a lot is going on in your mind. You then decide to watch a movie by one of the best actors and after a short time you find yourself completely engrossed on movie scenes. As you watch, you find yourself involved in laughing, getting excited or sad depending on the story line; as a result, your anxiety levels drop because of your new focus. Readjusting focus is very essential in relieving stress for inspiration to set back on own accord.

Looking around; wherever you are, look around for anything inspirational or anything that stands out. Anything you find that causes some 'emotion' might end up being a very good source of inspiration.

Not being too serious; you do not have read loads of inspirational quotes to stay inspired. Inspiration comes from within and should not be 'waited' for. Just be involved in other matters and maintain your focus. The most important thing is to attain both emotional and physical comfort via relaxation.

Not hunting for inspiration; trying

too hard to be inspired does one more harm than good. This is because it makes you end up with stress with nothing but sloppy ideas. It is, therefore, advisable not to overthink about anything. If you happen to have an idea of what keeps you inspired, do not try in any way to change or expand it, relax and keep it simple and in its current state.

II.   Create a flow of Inspiration

Consider the following

Enriching oneself; inspiration can be borne by simple ideas in one's mind. Try having as many ideas but remember not to try too hard or to overthink. You can also listen to inspirational music with inspiring lyrics or try something new to find out what works best for you.

Consider drawing on own resources; since concepts and ideas from your mind can turn out to be a great source of inspiration, think about any situation or circumstance that you feel strongly and positively about

III.   Capture Your Inspiration

Capturing your inspiration can be through;

Writing down ideas; this can be ideas previously thought about. Recall to previously interesting thoughts and analyze them deeply. A good example is thinking about the best form of transportation if you previously thought of getting around.

With the idea about what you find fascinating, emotional or interesting, close your eyes slowly and try to vividly create the picture in your mind. With this imagination, be keen on how you feel and if positive, try producing an outline on paper with different but related ideas. This is important in capturing the essence of your idea in trying to keep you inspired.

IV.   Stay on Track

Quitting is never an option if whatever you are trying to achieve gets hard. If you think you have had enough, just leave it and come to it later. Consequently, try to be organized and managing your time well. This is important in helping you get on top of your 'to do list.'

Setting achievable goals is the next step. What would you be proud achieving? Think about it and set daily habits to help you reach the ultimate goal. Meeting objectives should act as a good motivation for accomplishing bigger future goals.

Important tips for inspiration

• If your source of inspiration is from an individual, never copy his actions instead try to put yourself in the person's place and simulate the situation

• Always be honest with yourself,

this will help you achieve value from your creative product

• Always try to draw inspiration from within and not from emulating others

• Look at situations or circumstances with a positive inner eye and do not forget to write a sketch on any inspirational piece for remembrance.

Chapter Twelve

The Progression Habitat Models

"It is not true that there must be an example before you can attempt anything but never despise the power of a good example"

Some real life business stories on beating odds to become a reference point and outstanding success.

1. **A Downs syndrome Greeting card entrepreneur; Anna Rudick**

Anna Rudick was born with a Downs Syndrome condition. with many years of struggle and rejection even from the closest of friends, Ann only has her mentor and parents to thank for their support and courage to stand with her in the most challenging moments of her life.

One thing was for sure, she could not depend on her parents forever so she had to look for something unique to involve herself in, something she will consider as her own accomplishment; greeting cards entrepreneurship idea was therefore born

She could not manage to set up everything alone so she relied on some friends and disabled volunteers. *The greeting cards are handmade then customised with regard to each client's preference and sold through a website called Etsy.com*

Because of her condition, Anna Ruddick is not allowed to own assets of more than $2000 so most of her income is donated to charity to help people with the same disorder.

Currently the business enterprise boosts of lots of orders from over 50 states from all over the world and has created employment for lots of disabled people who initially had no hope in life.

"I was happy when she developed a

different perspective about life, that you can do anything and everything so long as you have a dream and committed to achieving it" her dad John Ruddick was once quoted.

2. Bet-David financial firm; Patrick Bet-David

Patrick Bet-David was born in 1970 in Iran a time when Iran was Experiencing Revolution war. in 1980 as a 10 year old, they managed to leave Iran with his mother for Germany where they spent two years in a refugee Camp after which he immigrated to the USA as a twelve year old.

He joined school and struggled to excel in all subjects except mathematics. Education struggles left him with no option other than joining the army almost immediately after high school.

The military job was not satisfactory, he bounced between jobs; as a gym instructor then in a financial firm where he worked his way up though he was not satisfied and decided to start his own business.

With experience in financial services, *he started his own firm in October 2009 providing life insurance, mutual funds and annuities*. Currently, the firm is ranked as one of the fastest growing with billions of dollars in transactions.

In an interview, Bet David once said; *"I did not know that I will reach such heights because firstly, as a child, parents cautioned their kids about me because they believed I could amount to nothing. I don't even have a four year degree and was hired at Morgan Stanley simply because my resume had a joke that made him laugh. The manager said that he had to meet this person and after the interview, I got the job which gave me the experience to be where I am. From the beginning and even as a kid in a refugee camp, I never stopped dreaming, I knew I would make it, I only had to keep going''*

3. Fingerprint Security-Pro App; Chad Mureta

Chad Mureta was one man who turned a tragedy into an empire. He had been involved in a near fatal car accident that left him bed ridden for quite a long time.

With a real estate business, Chad medical bills were soaring and therefore the real estate ventures could not support own operations and at the same time pay his high bills. It was a matter of time just before he could hit a dead end and so, he had to think of something else to substitute his declining real estate revenues

In bed and cut off from the outside world, Chad had access to magazines in the hospital. He came across one article on mobile apps and decided to give it a shot. Without any knowledge in programming, only with a pen and a piece of paper, he sketched his idea and outsourced his work from an app development company

With a *loan of $1800 the Fingerprint Security-Pro App was produced* and soon after, it was ranked among the best apps in App Store having racked up more than

$150,000 as soon as it was introduced. *The Empire Apps, T3 Apps and Best Apps* are products of Fingerprint Security-Pro apps and have also been well received in the market. *In total, 46 apps have been developed by Mureta and downloaded for more than 36million times.* He has also authored a book **"App Empire: Make Money, Have a Life, and Let Technology Work for you" (Wiley, 2012).**

Without knowledge and experience in technology, Mureta managed to succeed in app development. He says; *"I was never a tech guy when I started developing apps. Am still not a tech guy, I cannot tell you how to develop an app but if you ask me, I will tell you how to make it a success. I did a lot of market and consumer research and utilised the opportunities that I saw. Until now, I keep seeking knowledge to grow my business."*

4. Tandem Skydiving Business enterprise; John Cavaick Martin

Born in 1962, John Cavaick Martin's father was killed in an aircraft accident when he was eleven years old. Growing without someone he had looked up to as a child was not easy for him but he vowed to himself to keep his father's dreams alive. So, in 1979, at the age of 13, John Cavaick made his first parachute jump and by 1989, he had completed more than 600 parachute jumps and over 1500 flying hours.

Unfortunately, during this time, while on assignment, he also experienced a plane accident where he crashed and burnt. With 3rd degree burns, all-over his body, John spent three months in an induced Coma followed by unpleasant hospital appointments and treatments for four years.

On complete recovery, he returned to flying and set up his own skydiving business in the name of Tandem Skydiving Business. What kept him going was his never die attitude. Even with 25% chance of survival after crash burning, he was never depressed. His book *out of the ashes* is one of the best sales and his skydiving business has been overwhelming in recent years.

5.A wounded soldier who pursued

a dream;

Brian Kolfage stationed in Iraq, in an air base called Balad, a rocket exploded a few feet from where Brian Kolfage was standing. His limbs were completely destroyed and his life was on the edge having undergone sixteen surgeries. Now a triple amputee, Brian was discharged from hospital after twelve months.

After three years and with all but

prosthetic limbs, Brian Kolfage trained his non-dominant left hand and later on enrolled himself in the University of Arizona for a course in architecture where only talented and few applicants were accepted. He graduated in 2014 with *a 3.8 GPA and won a Pat Tillman Scholarship*. Brian Kolfage hopes to "<u>revolutionize architecture in military</u>" he was once quoted; *'even though I lost my limbs, I still have my head and brain and can therefore do everything I did before''*

6.A Graduating Janitor; Gac Filipaj

Gac Filipaj was a student in Colombia University's New York City campus. As a hustling undergraduate, he emptied garbage and cleaned floors for almost two decades. His shift usually ran from 2.30pm-5.00pm a time when fellow students were in class. But he had no option since that is where he raised his tuition fees from. Having immigrated to the USA in 1992 with no knowledge of English language, Gac Filipaj enrolled for up to two classes each semester and worked hard by studying well past midnight. He graduated at the age of 52 in May 2012 with honours. Gac Filipaj once said; *'I am happy to have fulfilled half of my dreams I look forward to completing it by going to graduate school''*

7. Limitless Curiosity of a Polio Victim; Martha Mason

In 1948, Martha mason was confined for 23 hours a day in a horizontal tube weighing approximately 800 pounds. At this time, she was eleven years and had been paralysed by polio and supported by an iron lung. Because of her 'endless curiosity', determination and focus to learn, *custom built intercoms* technology was utilised to connect her to her school right through to college where she majored in English. Unfortunately she passed on in the year 2009 having set a sixty year record with an iron lung. In her documentary *Martha in Lattimore*, she says; '*it sometimes happens to all of us, mine is more visible compared to yours but none of us is exempted from something that makes him extraordinary. Only if the world knew the story*''

8.A Refugee who opened a clinic; Jacob Atem

Atem's parents were killed in civil war when he was only six years of age, at the age of nine; he walked thousands of miles to Ethiopia from Sudan and settle in one of East Africa Refugee camps. His life in the camp did not end in vain as he was selected for an Orphans' programme in the USA.

Having not been in the USA before and not knowing a word in English only but motivated him. He later graduated with masters in English from *Michigan's Spring Arbor University* and there being inadequate healthcare services in his home country, he founded *the Southern Sudan Healthcare Organisation in the year 2008* after which he commenced with Ph.D.

studies in health services in the University of Florida. *He is still focused to gaining expertise that will make his clinic the 'model of the entire nation'*

9.A Great-grandma with a master's;Nola Ochs

A bachelor's degree is obtained in approximately for years.Nola Ochs sat in her first University class in the year *1930 at Kansas' Fort Hays State University*. Seventy seven years later aged 95 years old, Nola Ochs, a widowed grandmother then enrolled to complete her last thirty hours of art classes and history. She even moved to the campus apartments from her farm. *In the year 2010 and at the age of 98, she handed in a 50-paged research paper and not only excelled in her final exams but also qualified for a master's degree.*

10.Trapped in a car wreck for 5 days; Lindsay Thomas

Lindsey Thomas, a bartender in West Des Moines was driving *her 1989 ford escort* to her second job in Waverly, Iowa when she dozed off and *slammed into a concrete culvert beneath Interstate 35.*Calf deep in water with legs pinned below the shuttered dashboard with broken ribs, right wrist and jaw, Lindsey knew it was only a matter of time before she passed on.

Trapped for five days, she kept sipping water from a bottle she found in the car. She also napped and prayed. On the fifth day, it rained heavily and that made her feel colder and weaker. Her voice grew faint that nobody could hear her and for that reason, she gave up yelling.

Luckily, road workers saw tyre tracks and their curiosity led them to where Lindsey was trapped. She was rescued and airlifted to a University hospital in Iowa city where doctors confirmed that her legs had to be amputated.

A cyclist and a cross-country runner, Lindsay now hopes to complete college and pursue her dream in the design of prosthetics.

11.Liver transplant survivor; Rebecca Olch

While still a freshman at UC-Santa

Barbara, Rebecca Olch experienced prolonged vomiting bouts and was advised to see a family doctor. That night she was found collapsed on her bathroom floor by her parents.

Tests carried out confirmed that the parents were carriers of Wilson's disease; *a condition where the liver is unable to metabolize copper.* Copper had built up in Rebecca's system leading to liver shut down. Liver transplant was the only option but resulting complications caused it to fail and the lungs to haemorrhage. The doctor in charge said that she was seconds away from being confirmed dead then suddenly and against all odds the surgeons managed to stop the bleeding and soon after her condition improved.

A successful second transplant was carried out and even though she currently uses anti-rejection drugs, she likes unwinding in a Bikini revealing her surgical scar. She stated; *''this is what I only have to remind me of what happened''*

ABOUT THE AUTHOR

Adolph Obasogie is a Chartered Accountant and a member of prestigious professional bodies like the Institute of Chartered Accountants of Nigeria, Chartered Institute of Taxation of Nigeria, West African Insitute of Accounting Technicians, and the Chicago, Illinois-based Information Systems Audit and Control Association.

He resides in South Africa where he practices as a Life Coach, Author and Business Process Consultant.